20
16

Lake Effect Snow in Upstate New York

BY ANDRE J. GARANT

Lake Effect Phenomenon

The subject of lake effect snow has fascinated me ever since I was a young boy growing up on Long Island, New York. I would hear about it on TV or read about it in the local newspaper every once in a while, but never had the ability to experience it firsthand. I was a lover of snow, perhaps because Long Island received so little of it. With an average of 25 inches of snow in any given winter in my hometown of Port Jefferson, I longed for the white stuff every single day of the winter. When we had those rare "snow days", I was like a kid in a candy store, running outside with my film camera to snap memories of snow-covered branches and snowbanks along the side of the road. I simply couldn't get enough of snow and always wanted more of it. During my high school years, I dreamed about moving to Upstate New York when I was an adult, simply so I could see more snow. I read books about it, looked at pictures of it, but no matter what I did, I simply could not quench my thirst for SNOW!

Oddly enough, to this day nearly forty years later, I still never made the move to Upstate New York to satisfy my desire for snow, but that's okay with me. As an adult, the thrill has worn off to some extent, but I still do enjoy a good snowfall and especially since I am an avid landscape photographer. So, if you are reading this book, chances are you are a snow lover and someone who is interested in learning more about lake effect snow, primarily in Upstate New York. Therefore, it will be my job to pass along the knowledge I have gained on this subject, for I believe it is quite extensive. I have read numerous articles and books on the subject and have also accumulated a wealth of climate data on lake effect snow, so I do feel I know quite a bit about the subject. This book will not be overly scientific in nature with stuff only geeks can comprehend, but rather an account as seen through my eyes. After reading this book, you will have a general appreciation for lake effect snow as well as a basic knowledge on the subject.

Let's start off with describing what exactly lake effect snow is and how it differs from regular snow. First, in order to have lake effect snow, you must have several ingredients. Think about making a cake. In order to be successful, you must have the right ingredients, and exactly the proper amount of such ingredients. If you have too much sugar or not enough flour, the cake won't come out right. The same can be said about lake effect snow. The main ingredients needed for lake effect snow are cold air, warm water, wind, distance, and to a lesser extent, a sloping topography. Now that we have the ingredients mentioned, let's describe why each one is so vital to making the end result.

First off, you cannot have lake effect snow without cold air. Obviously, cold air is needed to make snow, so no cold air, no lake effect snow. Second, you cannot have lake effect snow without warm water in a large body of water such as a lake. When I say "warm water", I mean that it is several degrees warmer than the air above the lake. It could be 45 degrees, 50 degrees, or some other temperature as there is no set requirement on this. However, I should also note that the optimal temperature of the water is approximately 23 degrees warmer than the air blowing over it. So, if we have a temperature of 32 degrees outside, in order to produce heavy lake effect snow, the lake temperature would be as close to 55 degrees as possible, or warmer.

Next, you must have a light to moderate wind blowing over the top of the water in order to pick up the moisture content given off by the warm water. When cold air rushes down and meets up with the warm water, a lifting process occurs whereby the air picks up that moisture and brings it downstream according to the wind direction. As a general rule, the stronger the wind to a certain extent, the heavier the lake effect snow event will be, and this also determines how far the snow will travel. One caveat regarding this is that the wind should not exceed 30 miles per hour since this will limit the amount of moisture that can be picked up. The next ingredient needed is distance, also known as fetch.

Let's explain this one. Think of a large lake. If the process described above has thirty miles or more, the greater the amount of moisture that can be picked up. If the lake is only five miles long, the lake effect process just isn't possible because there is not enough distance for the moisture to be picked up and deposited downstream as snow. Last, the topography is very important since, in many cases, areas that are sloping in topography (i.e. hilly in nature) can receive more snow. This is because the nature of the wind blowing up against the higher elevation causes a process where more moisture is lifted up into the atmosphere and eventually deposited as snow. It should also be noted that the air travels slower once it reaches the land and this may in turn cause more snow to build up and be released in the atmosphere.

Now that we have the ingredients for lake effect snow mentioned, let's talk about some places in the world where this phenomenon is most common. Parts of Northern Japan are famous for lake effect snow (yes, Japan) as well as parts of Great Salt Lake in Utah. The Caspian and Black Seas are also famous for receiving lake effect snow, but perhaps the single most famous areas are the Great Lakes in the eastern United States. Think about what I wrote above, how the Great Lakes are very long and are therefore capable of producing lake effect snow, and especially due to the cold air masses which come sweeping down from Canada with strong winds that are famous for creating lake effect snow.

Two areas that can receive tremendous lake effect snow are Cleveland, Ohio as well as Erie, Pennsylvania. Both of these cities are situated at the far eastern end of Lake Erie and are ideally situated for all of the ingredients mentioned above to come together. Some areas of Lake Michigan are also noteworthy for lake effect snow, primarily areas on the southeastern shore, such as

Benton Harbor, Michigan and Michigan City, Indiana. Areas further inland such as Grand Rapids, Michigan and South Bend, Indiana are also famous for their locations within the "snow belt". Although Chicago is also situated on Lake Michigan, its location on the western side is not conducive for lake effect snow simply because the winds don't usually blow from east to west.

If the winds are blowing out of the north, however, areas on the extreme southern tip of Lake Michigan, such as Gary, Indiana, may be in the path of heavy, lake effect snow. The grand prize winner for lake effect snow, however, goes to the Keweenaw Peninsula of Northern Michigan where some places average well over 200 inches of snow per season. Such locations include

Marquette, Houghton, and Herman. In fact, Herman, Michigan has an average annual snowfall of 236 inches!

When talking about lake effect snow, there are two main distinguishing features that differentiate it from regular snow caused by a low-pressure system. The first is intensity and the second is locality. Lake effect snow is almost always very intense in the manner in which it falls since it can be extremely heavy and fall at the rate of five inches per hour (or more). Whiteout conditions are almost always associated with lake effect snow bands where visibility may be limited to less than fifty feet, and in extreme cases, as little as ten feet.

Locality is very important since lake effect snow is often

very isolated in that it can be snowing like crazy in one town, but just two miles away in another town, there will be no snow at all and the sun may even be shining. This is due to a process called "banding" which simply means that lake effect snow will often set up in long streamers or "bands" which may appear like fingers on a radar map. The wind direction will usually determine exactly where the snow falls, and when all of the ingredients come together, lake effect snow can fall in a long, narrow band that can extend for up to 100 miles in length, primarily from west to east depending on the wind direction and speed.

Another consideration I didn't mention yet regarding lake effect snow is that there is a distinct "season" when it typically occurs, and that season basically runs for about two months starting in late October and running until around Christmas. Let's use Lake Erie as an example. The first major lake effect snowfall will normally occur in early November as a strong cold front comes sweeping down from Canada. When the cold air mass hits the relatively mild lake, uplifting then occurs. If the wind direction is just right, the fetch causes moisture to lift into the atmosphere and fall as snow on the eastern, or lee, side of the lake.

The bullseye will often be Erie, Pennsylvania or Dunkirk, New York. As the season progresses, the lake water becomes colder and colder and is less able to support this uplifting process. If the weather becomes cold enough in January, the lake eventually freezes over and the so-called lake effect snow machine is now shut off. It is impossible for lake effect snow to occur once the body of water has frozen over. During very cold winters, such as 2013-14, Lake Erie froze over relatively quickly and the lake effect snow season was quite short. However, during the milder winter of 2015-16, the lake never completely froze solid, and therefore the lake effect snow phenomenon was possible all winter long. When looking back at some of the most noteworthy lake effect snow events, many of them have occurred in November or December, but this is not always the case as there have been other severe ones in October, January and February.

Now, let's talk about the locations in Upstate New York that are known for lake effect snow. If you were to walk down any street in Manhattan and ask folks where they thought the snowiest place in New York would be, nine out of ten would say "Buffalo". This is simply false! Although Buffalo has had its share of very heavy lake effect snowfalls, this city is simply not in what I refer to as the "bullseye" of lake effect snow. There are two such "bullseyes" or core areas in New York where lake effect snow is both common and intense. The first area is that of the famous Tug Hill Plateau, a very isolated, remote area located just east of Lake Ontario and northeast of Syracuse. The second is a narrow area located about ten miles inland from the shores of Lake Erie in southwestern New York. This area runs roughly forty miles long by fifteen miles wide and starts near Hamburg, New York and runs south to just north of Jamestown, New York. Both of these areas receive an average of 175 inches of snow per year, and often much more!

When talking about cities in Upstate New York that receive lake effect snow, the answer is several of them, but let's take a closer look at this. Buffalo, with an average snowfall of 94 inches per year, is on the low end and I will talk about why in just a minute. Rochester often averages around 100 inches per year, but the winner hands down goes to Syracuse which receives an average of 116 inches of snow each winter, and is also acclaimed to be the snowiest large city in the Continental United States. Heading further east down the

New York Thruway, the snowfall rates drop off substantially to just 80 inches per year in Utica and then closer to 60 inches in Albany. The reason why is location! In order to understand this more closely, pick up a map of New York and look at the location of each of these cities. Buffalo, although situated on Lake Erie, is located at the far northeastern tip. This puts the city too far north to be in the path of heavy lake effect snow, simply because the wind often blows from northwest to southeast, thereby putting towns further down the lake in a much heavier snow location. This is why Dunkirk and Fredonia often receive much more in the way of lake effect snow.

Next, take a look at Rochester. Its location just to the south of Lake Ontario puts it too far south and also too far west to be in the path of heavy lake effect snow. Unless the wind is blowing directly from the north, Rochester will not be in the path of heavy lake effect snow. Now, when looking at the location of Syracuse, however, we have a much more favorable location for heavy lake effect snow. This is because Syracuse, although farther inland, lies just to the southeast of Lake Ontario.

With the strong, cold winds from Canada often blowing from northwest to southeast, look at the incredible distance of the lake that the air has to travel over before it reaches the eastern shores near Oswego and Mexico. Previously, I described this as fetch. This location is very favorable for heavy, lake effect snow. In fact, the two small cities of Fulton and Oswego, New York are probably the first and second snowiest small cities in the entire United States with average snowfalls of 140 inches or more per year! While Oswego is located right on the southeast shore of Lake Ontario, Fulton is about 15 miles inland.

Further east, although Utica and Albany are not located near a lake which can produce lake effect snow, streamers or bands that form can often hold together long enough to reach Utica, and in more rare instances, the Capital Region of Albany, Schenectady, and Troy. This all depends on wind direction and wind speed. Although other cities in Upstate New York can receive lake effect snow, it is often much less in amount and frequency. Such cities include Auburn, Cortland,

Ithaca, Binghamton, and Watertown. Annual snowfall for these cities is in the range of 70-100 inches per year, but they are also affected by low pressure systems. This is especially true of Binghamton, which is situated far enough south and east to pick up heavy snow from storms that travel up the east coast, but is also located far enough north and west to pick up lake effect snow from bands or streamers that hold together far enough inland.

Binghamton, with an average annual snowfall of 86 inches, is one of the snowiest cities in Upstate New York. However, this can be confusing since weather records are kept at Binghamton Regional Airport, which is located in the hilly terrain north of the city at an elevation close to 1,600 feet, and this certainly can lead to more snow than what would fall down in the Susquehanna River Valley where the actual city of Binghamton is located, and also at an elevation closer to 850 feet. Elevation alone in this part of New York can make the difference between 60 inches of snow per winter down in the river valleys versus 90 inches on the surrounding hilltops.

The Tug Hill Plateau

As previously mentioned, the Tug Hill Plateau is a typical hot spot for lake effect snow to occur in Upstate New York. If you are not already familiar with this area, it might be best to do some reading on it. Wikipedia is always a great place to start, and simply describes this area as a large "cuesta" comprised of sedimentary rock that tips up on one side, rising from approximately **350** feet in elevation on the west side and sloping up to around **2,000** feet in elevation on the east side. Therefore, this area of land is not truly a plateau, but rather a cuesta, best described as a hill or ridge with a gentle slope on one side and a much steeper slope on the opposite side. In order to see this, it is best to consult a topographical map which shows the contours of the land. This also explains why the Tug Hill is home to a few ski areas which are located on the far eastern side near the Black River Valley.

Let's also take a look at the Tug Hill since it is a huge area that comprises approximately 2,100 square miles and encompasses 41 towns spread across the four different counties of Jefferson, Lewis, Oneida, and Oswego. Wow! Next, let's consider that the Tug Hill actually has an inner "core" area which is where the most remote forests are located with very few roads. What roads do exist are often narrow and unpaved, and very few people live in this area. Most of it is now owned by the State of New York, but one can also find occasional privately owned hunting camps and seasonal lodges.

This inner core of the Tug Hill Plateau is comprised of very poor soil that is not conducive to growing crops, and if that is not bad enough, the growing season is extremely short. There are numerous rivers, streams, and creeks that traverse the area. As one might imagine, this nature lover's paradise is home to a large wildlife population which includes deer, black bear, coyotes, bobcats, beavers, and a whole host of others. Today, the Tug Hill is famous for its spectacular recreational opportunities, the first of which is snowmobiling during the winter. With ample snowfall that often exceeds 200 inches per season, it is rare to come to this area in the winter and find that there is not enough snow to enjoy these famous wintertime activities. In fact, if one travels to the Tug Hill region during the winter, you might find the snow to be three, four, or even five feet deep! One interesting phenomenon about this area is to find hunting lodges that have doors on the second floor. This is simply to allow entry after the snow becomes so deep that the doors on the first floor are completely buried!

If one word can best describe the Tug Hill Plateau, it might be "snowy". Now, let's pick up that road map of New York State once again and see where this area exactly is located. If your map is small enough, you might see a strange bare spot located about 35 miles northeast of Syracuse and 15 miles southeast of Watertown. It is pretty much hemmed in by Interstate 81 and Route 11 on the west side, Route 13 on the south side, Route 26 on the east side, and Route 12 on the north side. There are no cities in the Tug Hill Plateau and very few towns that have more than a few hundred residents. If you glance at your map, check out the location of Lake Ontario to the west. This massive lake, named the 14th largest in the world, has a maximum length of 193 miles from west to east.

At the far southeastern tip lies Oswego, and just to the east of that spot, the lake then curves northward near the town of Ramona Beach. The massive size of Lake Ontario is what contributes to some very impressive lake effect snowfalls, which often fall anywhere from

Oswego in the south to Watertown in the north. If the wind is blowing due east, the snow bands target the Tug Hill Plateau, explaining why this part of New York is what we call the "bullseye" of lake effect snow events.

If one were to do some research on the snowiest towns in New York State, those located inside the Tug Hill Plateau would easily be in the top ten. Some of the ones that top the list include Redfield, Barnes Corners, Montague, Hooker, and High Market, just to name a few. In fact, the record for the most snow in one winter (for the state of New York) goes to Hooker which received a whopping 476 inches of snow during the winter of 1976-77! When it comes to a daily record, that award goes to Montague which received an incredible 77 inches of snow within a 24-hour period back in January of 1997! But, the list goes on with some of the more recent lake effect snow events. Back in February of 2007, one of the most intense lake effect snow events took place where an unbelievable 141 inches of snow fell on Redfield during a span of ten days, and an equally impressive 121 inches fell on Parish. Even North Osceola got in on the action, which received 106 inches of snow between February 3rd and February 12th of that year.

One can now easily understand why the Tug Hill Plateau has been deemed the "Snow Capital of the World." In fact, locals often describe certain lake effect snow events as "the most intense storms in the world" where visibility can be cut to zero in blinding snow and high winds where snowfall rates of six inches or more per hour are not uncommon and also accompanied by thunder and lightning. During more severe winters, it is also possible to have more than five feet of snow on the ground at any one time!

One of my favorite childhood books is one titled *Snow Bound* by Harry Mazer, which was originally published in 1974. It tells the fictional tale of young Tony LaPorte who decides to take off in his family's car for a joyride during a snowy winter day in Syracuse, New York. Tony heads north on Interstate 81 and runs into a very heavy snow squall near Sandy Creek. After exiting the highway and taking Route 11, he picks up Cindy Reichert, a hitchhiker on the side of the road and the two eventually get lost somewhere inside the Tug Hill Plateau on a lonely road during an intense lake effect snowstorm. To make a long story short, the two end up snowbound in the car for several days with only a small supply of cookies and nearly die from the extreme cold and desolation. The story supposedly takes place near Redfield, and after a long struggle to survive, the two are rescued when they eventually find a nearby home.

This story may sound exaggerated, but such an event could very likely happen in the Tug Hill Plateau during an extreme lake effect snow event that can last several days. If one decides to travel in or near this area during the winter months, it is best to be prepared for such an event where a sudden snow squall

can change the landscape in a
matter of minutes and leave one
stranded and hanging on for dear
life.

Southwestern New York State

The second "bullseye" for lake effect snow in New York is the extreme southwestern corner in the counties of Chautauqua, Cattaraugus, and Erie. As I described earlier, this is a long band extending roughly 40 miles from southwest to northeast and about 10-15 miles wide where the heaviest lake effect snow will often fall during lake effect snow events associated with Lake Erie. If a person pays close attention to locations often mentioned during severe lake effect snow events in western New York, one might hear towns such as Orchard Park, Hamburg, and Blasdell mentioned.

If one glances at a map, the long stretch of Lake Erie lies directly to the west, and if the cold, winter winds are set up just right, these towns will get hammered with extremely heavy, lake effect snow that can last for days at a time. Let's take a gander at Lake Erie real quickly. Wikipedia describes it as being 241 miles long at its maximum point and 57 miles wide. With an average depth of just 62 feet, it is the shallowest of the five Great Lakes, which also makes it the warmest lake of the group. This might also explain why the lake is such a hot spot for lake effect snow. If the winter winds set up in a southwestern to northeastern fashion, the heaviest lake effect snow will fall in Buffalo, but just a slight shift in wind direction can pull the heavy snow bands farther south.

Starting with Chautauqua County, this is New York State's

westernmost county which borders
Lake Erie on the west, Erie County
to the north, Cattaraugus County
to the east, and Pennsylvania on
the south. The largest city is
Jamestown with 31,000 residents,
which is a very snowy area prone
to frequent lake effect snow
events, some of which can be
paralyzing. Dunkirk, the second
largest "city" in this county, is
situated directly on Lake Erie and
is in the "bullseye" of very heavy
lake effect snow, as is Fredonia, of
similar size and situated just a few
miles inland.

When the lake effect snow
begins to fly in November each
year, one will often see these two
towns featured on the Weather
Channel with blinding snow falling
nearly horizontally. Interstate 90,
also known as the New York
Thruway, will often be temporarily

closed in this area due to the blowing and drifting snow. Chautauqua County is a beautiful spot in New York with rolling hills that average between 1,100 feet and 2,000 feet in elevation. The elevation alone will contribute to more lake effect snow, which is why the highest totals tend to be in the eastern portion of the county as this is where the highest elevations will be. Five of the snowiest towns in Chautauqua County are Dunkirk, Silver Creek, Ripley, Mayville, and Cassadaga.

To the east lies Cattaraugus County, an area known for incredibly heavy lake effect snow. The terrain here tends to be more rugged with the rolling hills giving way to small mountains, some of which make for great ski areas that include Holiday Valley Resort in Ellicottville. With long, cold and very snowy winters, these areas benefit from Mother Nature who can dump as much as 250 inches of snow on the highest elevations in a single season. Although Cattaraugus County is 99% rural with many narrow, dirt roads, the one small city of Olean is home to 15,000 residents. One of the interesting tidbits about this remote part of New York is a concentrated population of Amish folk who reside in the western portion of Cattaraugus County and who live without indoor plumbing and modern day conveniences.

Most people know that a very large concentration of Amish live in the Lancaster area of Pennsylvania, but there are quite a few also located in western New York who prefer the more rugged terrain as well as an area not yet infested by tourists, etc. If I were to name the snowiest towns in Cattaraugus County, I would mention Little Valley, Ellicottville, Otto, Randolph, and Cattaraugus.

The last county mentioned in this "bullseye" is Erie County, which is also where Buffalo is located. The extreme southern portions of this county are by far the snowiest and include the towns of Angola, Eden, North Boston, and Springville. However, areas just a bit farther north are also within the "bullseye" and include Hamburg, Orchard Park, East Aurora, and Wales. These communities are all suburbs of Buffalo and home to thousands of residents. The way that lake effect snow bands will set up in the winter will determine whether these towns receive a mere dusting or get buried under 80 inches of snow.

Such a phenomenon occurred during the freak November storm in 2014 that I will talk about later in this book. Sometimes a distance of a mile can make the difference between using your broom to clear the front stoop or having to break out the snow blower and contend with several feet of dry, powdery snow. As one moves to the northern sections of Erie County, lake effect snow totals drop off significantly and are lowest along the border with Niagara County. Towns within this boundary include Amherst, Akron, Clarence, and Tonawanda, but even these areas can receive significant lake effect snow, again depending on the exact wind direction and set up of lake effect bands.

The Golden Snowball Award

This special award is given
to the city in Upstate New York
that receives the most snow in any
one season. There are five cities
that currently compete in this fun
event, which are Albany, Buffalo,
Binghamton, Rochester, and
Syracuse. Frankly, I am not sure
why Albany participates since it
has never won the award and, as
mentioned earlier, is not in an
area conducive to lake effect
snow. There is a great article on
Wikipedia about this event which
shows a table depicting the
amount of snow that each city has
received for the past seventy or so
years. It is very interesting to
study these numbers, for if you
are a lover of snow stats like I am,
this will light up your eyes.
Although only five major cities
now participate in the event, it

formerly included other smaller cities such as Fulton, Oswego, Utica, and Watertown. I am pretty sure that Fulton or Oswego would top the list in pretty much any given season due to its strategic location on Lake Ontario. When looking at the results of past years, Syracuse is almost always the winner, although Rochester took first place during the winter of 2011-12. Albany usually comes in dead last since it is not subject to lake effect snow, and set the record for the least snow received in any one season with just a mere 14 inches during the winter of 1912-13.

When looking more closely at the stats, here are the greatest and lowest amounts of snow in any given season by location; Albany, 113 inches in 1970-71, 14 inches in 1912-13; Binghamton, 134 inches in 1995-96, 44 inches in 2011-12; Buffalo, 199 inches in 1976-77, 37 inches in 2011-12; Rochester, 162 inches in 1959-60, 42 inches in 1952-53; Syracuse, 192 inches in 1992-93, 51 inches in 2011-12. These stats show some interesting information. The winter of 2011-12 was one of the least snowy in Upstate New York and was very mild overall. The winter of 1995-96 where Binghamton had its snowiest winter was very snowy across New England and much of the snow that Binghamton received was not from lake effect, but rather low pressure systems moving up the East Coast.

Another very snowy winter across central and eastern New York was in 1992-93, where in December of 1992, a paralyzing snowstorm occurred from central

New York over into central New England where some locations received up to 40 inches across The Berkshires of western Massachusetts. This was the snowiest winter on record in Syracuse with 192 inches and also a whopping 123 inches in Binghamton!

The winter of 1976-77 was overall a bitterly cold and snowy winter across Upstate New York which brought Buffalo its greatest snowfall total of any winter with 199 inches. Although Rochester "only" received 92 inches that season, Syracuse picked up 145 inches. The variation in totals is mainly due to where the lake effect snow bands set up. It does seem that very cold and snowy winters occur in cycles and we have had some noteworthy winters just recently. The winter of 2014-

15 was one of the coldest and snowiest on record in Upstate New York and started off with a behemoth lake effect snow event during the third week of November where some towns to the east and south of Buffalo received nearly 90 inches of snow over the period of a week. It was covered extensively on the news all over the country.

I will write more about this later, but this particularly cold and snowy winter dropped 113 inches on Buffalo, 102 inches on Rochester, and 120 inches in Syracuse. Some of the biggest snowfall totals occurred across central and eastern New York where Binghamton picked up 93 inches and Albany 76 inches. This particular winter came in as the snowiest on record in Boston where over 100 inches fell, and a

good chunk of it came during a
three-week stretch from late
January into the middle of
February. This was strictly due to
low-pressure systems moving up
the East Coast which targeted
much of southern and eastern New
England.

With some bitterly cold and
snowy winters, you also have some
very mild and dry winters, such as
what occurred in 2011-12.
During that particular winter, a
mere 37 inches fell in Buffalo, a
wimpy 51 inches in Syracuse, and
Rochester actually received the
most snow that season with 60
inches. Even places not normally
subject to lake effect snow had a
very snowless winter with only 44
inches falling in Binghamton and
just a meek 23 inches in Albany.
Just the winter before, however,
the story was much different with

a mammoth 179 inches falling in Syracuse during the winter of 2010-11, which proved to be one of the snowiest across much of Upstate New York. Even those areas not subject to much in the way of lake effect snow received very heavy snowfall in 2010-11, as 87 inches fell in Albany and 118 inches in Binghamton. By comparison, Buffalo received 112 inches and Rochester 127 inches.

By now, you are probably getting a good sense of how much snow Upstate New York can receive in any one winter. The fact of the matter is if you don't like snow, you don't live in Upstate New York year round, but if you do love snow, you have chosen wisely. It is important to note, however, that Upstate New York can have wonderful summers with warm days and cool nights, and very rarely does the temperate top 90 degrees. So, if you are willing to endure a cold and snowy winter, the rest of the year can be quite nice with very pleasant weather conditions. And.....virtually all of Upstate New York is amazingly beautiful in the Fall when the foliage turns!

The Blizzard of 1977

Now that I have given a good introduction to what lake effect snow is and how it occurs, I want to mention three specific weather events that are famous in the book of New York weather history. The first is the notorious Blizzard of 1977 which targeted western New York and parts of southern Ontario. But first, let me give a prelude to this incredible weather event by stating that the winter of 1976-77 was perhaps one of the coldest on record across western New York. The first snowfall occurred in the Buffalo suburb of Cheektowaga on October 9, which was a foreshadowing of what was to come later in the season. Just twelve days later, the area saw its first accumulating snow, with some areas picking up nearly a foot. The month ended with very chilly weather and the temperature of Lake Erie was already down below 50 degrees, a record for so early in the season. November was a very cold month in and around Buffalo and ended with an average temperature of 34 degrees, more than ten degrees below where it should have been. Snow fell on several days, especially late in the month where Buffalo picked up 19 inches on the 30th and the city ended the month with 31 inches. This was quite impressive for so early in the season, but some areas to the south of Buffalo picked up even more, and in some cases, up to four feet for the month!

The cold, snowy pattern continued in December where the average temperature for the month came in at 22 degrees in Buffalo, which was again at least ten degrees colder than average. It snowed nearly every single day in December and the total came in right around 60 inches for the month. A maximum snow depth of approximately 30 inches occurred at the beginning of the month, oddly enough. By the middle of December, Lake Erie had frozen over, which was the earliest date on record. Now, in most cases, this would be a good sign to Buffalo residents since it means the lake effect snow machine is simply shut off and no more lake effect snow will fall.

However, as one would quickly find out, this was not necessarily a good thing back in late 1976. Most residents of western New York figured that the cold weather would break and January wouldn't be so bad, but to the contrary, the cold and snowy weather in January intensified to no end. The average temperature for the month came in just shy of 14 degrees, which was the coldest since records started being kept in 1870! Another noteworthy milestone occurred that month, which was that the temperature never rose above freezing for the entire month, and it was the first time this had ever happened.

As if the severe cold was not bad enough, the snow continued in full force and fell nearly every single day in January, reaching a maximum depth of 59 inches on January 27th. I'm not sure most people realize just how deep this, but for the average adult, the snow would be up to your neck! By this day, the total snow that had fallen thus far in Buffalo for the winter was 151 inches, a crippling amount! And then....it happened, the famous Blizzard of 1977 struck the city! On Friday, January 28, a severe arctic front began crossing the Midwest states and made its way towards western New York. Along with the passage of the arctic front was a so-called "wall of snow" that dropped several inches of snow in just one hour on cities like Columbus, Ohio and Indianapolis, Indiana.

The temperature dropped nearly 25 degrees in just one hour! It should also be noted that due to the record-breaking cold weather for the past several months, Lake Erie was not only completely frozen over, but also covered with several feet of fine, powdery snow, something that would soon become the worst nightmare for every single resident of Buffalo, New York. With the arctic front now closing in on the city of 460,000 residents, winds began blowing at 30-40 miles per hour with gusts approaching 65 miles per hour. By 11:00 that Friday morning in late January of 1977, residents working in Buffalo's tallest skyscrapers noticed a wall of white closing in on the city from Lake Erie to the west.

Like a sudden summer thunderstorm, the storm struck Buffalo like a bat out of hell! Heavy, wind-driven snow began falling and created whiteout conditions within minutes. In addition to the heavy snow falling from the sky associated with the arctic cold front, the strong winds whipping across Lake Erie picked up tons of snow and began mixing that with the snow falling from the sky to create the perfect storm that every Buffalo resident alive at the time can still remember with vivid memories. By 11:30, the arctic front continued its eastward march and had passed through the Buffalo-Niagara International Airport, stranding planes on the tarmac as well as causing cars and trucks on Interstate 90 to become stuck in the snow.

Abandoned cars clogged city streets, preventing plows and emergency vehicles from getting through. People had no way to get home but walk, and this also became nearly impossible due to the blinding snow, strong winds, and bitter cold. Speaking of the temperature, what had started out as a normal January morning around 25 degrees soon became life threatening as the actual temperature plummeted to near zero degrees with the passage of the front, and with the winds blowing as strong as they were, the wind chill approached 60-70 degrees below zero! Exposed skin was subject to frostbite in a matter of just a few minutes.

The snow continued to rage right through the day and well into Friday night where nearly all roads were now impassable by drifts up to ten feet high. Thousands of people were stranded in downtown Buffalo with no way to get home, and in the suburbs, thousands of other workers were stranded at their workplaces and prepared to endure a night from hell. The Buffalo Police Department pleaded for help from residents who had snowmobiles and four-wheel drive vehicles so that they could maneuver around the city, and with all the chaos going on, looting also broke out in some areas of the city. There were widespread power outages and people had no idea how they would survive a night of extreme cold in the dark.

It was estimated that nearly 10,000 cars were stranded in the city of Buffalo alone, with thousands of others out in the suburbs which created a real hazard since snowplows could not see them due to the incredibly high snowdrifts. By the time Saturday morning finally rolled around, the storm began to let up after dropping approximately 12 inches of "new" snow, but it appeared to be much, much more than that due to the snow that had been picked up off of frozen Lake Erie and deposited on the area. The temperature had also dropped to a record low of -7 that night

and winds had gusted to a
maximum speed of 69 miles per
hour, creating wind chills that
some folks had never experienced
before. Cars had become
completely buried under
mountains of white, powdery snow,
and those that were not simply
refused to start due to dead
batteries. The engine
compartments and wheel wells of
cars were also filled with snow
which created additional
problems.

The Blizzard of 1977
continued to cause problems for
several days after the initial event
simply due to strong winds that
continued to pummel the area and
drift the snow into huge banks and
create near zero visibility at
times. The entire Buffalo region
was declared a Federal disaster
area by President Jimmy Carter

and the National Guard was deployed to all of western New York to help clean up the snow and also go door to door to find people who were trapped in their homes. It was reported that snow drifts were up to the roofs on many homes throughout the region, preventing anyone from getting out. It took all of a week, if not ten days, to get folks out of their homes and many roads remained impassable for days upon days. Buffalo remained under a state of emergency for several days after the blizzard, preventing anyone from unnecessary travel without facing huge fines.

In the aftermath of the famous blizzard, local meteorologists reported drifts as high as 30 feet, and in most cases, huge earth-moving equipment needed to be brought in to dig out nearly every road that was blocked by 10-20 foot snowdrifts. Snowbanks on the sides of roads reached well over 25 feet and made travel nearly impossible. In all, 23 people died in western New York from the Blizzard of 1977, with 11 of those just in the city of Buffalo itself. A few months later when Mother Nature finally released her grip on Buffalo, the city had recorded a staggering 199 inches of snow for the season, a record that continues to stand to this very day! For those residents of Buffalo who lived through this storm, it will surely be one they will remember for the rest of their lives!

The Buffalo Snowstorm of October 2006

One of the most astounding weather events to ever occur in Buffalo was that of the famous early-season snowstorm on October 12th and 13th back in 2006. Thursday, October 12th was much like any other typical October day in the Buffalo area, but some of the weather forecasters were warning of a possible lake effect snow event. Buffalo residents shunned this notion, believing the weather was simply too warm for such an event so early in the season. Early that morning, light rain began to fall throughout the area which continued all morning long.

By noon, the temperature at Buffalo-Niagara International Airport was a chilly 41 degrees,

even cold by Buffalo standards.
The first few wet snowflakes and
sleet pellets began to mix in with
the pesky rain shortly thereafter
as a mass of cold air began to
envelop the city. By 1:30, the
temperature continued to drop
and was now down to 36 degrees.
It appeared that as the rain fell, it
continued to cool down the upper
levels of the atmosphere and a
heavy, wet snow was soon to
arrive.

Weather forecasters in the
area were now scratching their
chins and decided it was time to
change the forecast and call for
snow, where some meteorologists
were predicting a heavy, wet
accumulation that could reach as
much as six inches throughout the
area. Residents still shook their
heads and said it wouldn't happen.
All of the trees in the area were

still approaching peak color as the leaves turned shades of red, orange, and yellow. With Halloween still over two weeks away, many residents felt that snow was the last thing that could affect their daily plans.

Shortly after 2:00, the weather continued to worsen as the precipitation changed over to all snow with a temperature of 34 degrees. The snow was now beginning to fall quite heavily, reducing visibility on the New York State Thruway to a half mile or less which already began to slow traffic to less than 25 miles per hour. Roadways remained mainly wet as the ground was still quite warm, but gradually, the ground began to turn white, and once it did, the game was on! The National Weather Service had now changed their tune and the entire area was placed under a lake effect snow warning starting at 8:00 PM with the likelihood of downed power lines and tree damage.

As the cold air continued to spill down from the atmosphere and mixed with the warm water of Lake Erie, conditions began to deteriorate even more and the snow grew heavier and heavier. By 5:00, many of the grassy areas were now snow-covered and even some of the secondary roads became covered with a slushy, white cement. As nightfall approached, thunder and lightning knocked on the door, and by 6:45, some areas were now covered with as much as three inches of heavy, wet snow. The National Weather Service changed the lake effect snow warning to be in effect immediately and warned that there would likely be extensive power outages and tree limbs down due to the weight of the snow on the trees.

As most Buffalo residents hunkered down and went to sleep that Thursday night, it continued to snow, and snow, and SNOW! By the time the morning of Friday, October 13th rolled around, much of Buffalo woke up to a world of white outside the window with no power. Up to 27 inches of snow ended up falling in some areas to the north and east of downtown and it was clear to see that the forecasters messed up the forecast and were way too conservative with their previous estimates. Due to the relatively warm ground, much of the snow that fell compacted and made the accumulations look less, but what was there was very heavy in consistency and felt like white cement when it was shoveled. It was estimated that 400,000 people were without power, and nearly a quarter of those would remain that way for as long as a week.

An unbelievable 13 people died from the snowstorm, some from automobile accidents and others from either falling trees on their houses or shoveling snow. Tree damage was so extensive that it was later estimated that 90% of the trees in the city of Buffalo had some sort of damage. Although all of the snow had melted by Tuesday, October 17th, the damage left behind was incredible, causing many Buffalo residents to describe the freak snowstorm as devastating and horrific.

When it was all said and done, the snow tallies published by the National Weather Service were quite impressive. This time around, the heaviest amounts were to the north and east of downtown Buffalo (as opposed to the south) where places like Alden and Depew received the jackpot of 24 inches. Cheektowaga received an impressive 23 inches while Amherst and Clarence received an average of 18 inches each. The Buffalo-Niagara International Airport received a whopping 22 inches, making it the sixth heaviest 24-hour snowfall for the airport, no matter what time of year.

Downtown Buffalo was not spared either, and had reported as much as 15 inches near the SUNY downtown campus. West Seneca and Tonawanda came in with 14 inches apiece while Hamburg reported nearly a foot. Even places farther to the east, such as Batavia in Genesee County, reported up to 10 inches. Farther north, Medina and Lockport both received in the vicinity of 8 inches. Virtually no town or village in western New York was spared as measurable snow was reported all the way to the western suburbs of Rochester. The October snowstorm of 2006 will go down in the history books as the earliest significant snowfall on record in the Buffalo area, and will likely remain that way for a long time.

Snowvember 2014

Perhaps the most significant lake effect snow event of all time was one which occurred over a four-day span between November 17th and November 20th back in 2014. This event severely pummeled the western New York region from Buffalo south to the Pennsylvania border with unprecedented snow totals which, in some cases, approached 90 inches! Nicknames such as "knife", "snowcopalypse", and "snowvember" were dished out. The storm was so enormous that it required more manpower than any other snow event in order to clear the snow and restore life to its normal balance. The heaviest snow fell approximately twenty miles east of Buffalo in a small town called Cowlesville, which tallied a massive 88 inches of snow! South Cheektowaga reported a crippling 65 inches! Keep in mind that Thanksgiving was still over a week away, so although heavy lake effect snow events are not uncommon in this part of New York during the month of November, none of them had dropped 88 inches before!

The pandemonium started on November 16th in the Buffalo area as forecasters warned of heavy, lake effect snow. The water temperature in Lake Erie was a somewhat balmy 48 degrees, perfect for producing heavy snow as the arctic air descended southeast from the Great Lakes region. Some weather forecasters could see the writing on the wall as all of the necessary ingredients were coming together to produce a massive lake effect snow event where final totals of three feet or more were looking very likely. By Monday evening, November 17th, light snow began falling across areas east of Lake Erie, primarily in areas just to the South of Buffalo that are more commonly referred to as "the southtowns". What began as light snow quickly became heavy with reported thunder and lightning as well. The snow began to form a narrow band about twenty miles wide which focused on the areas from Lackawanna eastward to Alden. The snow continued during the night with accumulations of 3-6 inches per hour, and by Tuesday morning, some locations had received as much as three feet of new snow!

The "jackpot" of snow was confined to this narrow band stretching from Lackawanna in the west to Alden in the east, but areas to the south also picked up quite a bit of snow, with up to one foot reported in Orchard Park and Attica. During the day on Tuesday, the lake effect snow band became extremely tight and could be seen as a wall of snow. One may remember seeing videos on TV where the snow produced a narrow "wall" of white coming in off of Lake Erie. Areas to the north, such as Lockport and Amherst, were practically sunny, and if one was flying in a plane, this distinct shield of snow was extremely impressive.

In fact, on Transit Road (Route 78), one could be driving down the road under sunny skies, while just two miles to the south, areas were in a complete whiteout with snow falling at the rate of five inches per hour! On Tuesday, the

New York Thruway was completely shut down from the Pennsylvania border all the way to Rochester, which basically stranded travelers in their cars on the road as heavy snow and strong winds pummeled the area. Tractor trailers were stuck on the road and prepared to spend a day or two gridlocked in the snow. One of these trucks was carrying all of the equipment for an upcoming New England Patriots game.

The snow and wind continued to rage during Tuesday night and finally began to let up by early Wednesday morning. By this time, there was so much snow on the ground in areas to the east and south of Buffalo that residents were completely trapped inside their homes. Pictures of the snow began to infiltrate the media and folks around the world marveled at this incredible snow event taking place in western New York! In some cases, homeowners would open their front doors and find snow piled up all the way to the roof.

In the days that ensued, residents of Buffalo and the surrounding suburbs did everything they could to try and clear the heavy snow away from their homes, but in some instances it proved to be too much as roofs began to cave in. A few days after the snow finally subsided, warmer weather moved into the region, and then there was the forecast of rain and melting snow which could create dangerous and deadly flood conditions. Thankfully, this never happened and the snow melted slow enough to avoid troublesome flooding.

In looking back at this event, meteorologists studied the conditions which led up to this infamous snowstorm and came to the conclusion that when every single ingredient comes together to produce massive lake effect snow, the end result was "snowcopalypse 2014". The fetch over Lake Erie was exactly right to produce the most favorable conditions for heavy, lake effect snow to form right over Buffalo and its southern suburbs. Every single ingredient was absolutely perfect from the wind direction to the wind speed to the lake temperature, and so on.

But perhaps what was so interesting was how narrow the snow band really was, and for how long it lasted. In most cases, lake effect snow is not so severely "cut off" and well defined as it was in this event. But Lake Erie was not the only place to receive heavy snow during that week back in November of 2014. Lake Ontario was also affected, though not nearly as bad. Areas to the east of the lake, such as the Tug Hill Plateau, reported up to two feet of snow with the heaviest accumulation of 22 inches measured in Philadelphia, New York. A general 12-18 inches were reported across most other towns, such as Redfield and Sandy Creek.

November of 2014 was just a foreshadowing of a horribly cold and snowy winter for much of Upstate New York. The good news was that Buffalo received the majority of its seasonal snowfall that winter during the month of November, but ended up with 113 inches for the season. Final snow tallies (provided courtesy of The Weather Channel) for the November 2014 "snowcopalypse" included 88 inches at Cowlesville, 74 inches at Lancaster, 71 inches at Orchard Park, 69 inches at Wales Center, 52 inches at West Seneca, 17 inches at the Buffalo-Niagara International Airport, and just 8 inches at Tonawanda, which was indicative of the sharp cut-off for areas just north of Buffalo. It will certainly be a month that all Buffalonians will remember for the rest of their lives!

Other Snowy Areas in Upstate New York

So far in this book, I have primarily talked about lake effect snow, and that's a good thing since that is what the title says the book is about. However, there are many other snowy areas in New York State that are not necessarily affected by lake effect snow, so let's briefly discuss those locations. The two distinct areas are the higher elevations of the Adirondack Mountains and Catskill Mountains. The theme here is elevation! So, it would be a very true statement to say that the areas in Upstate New York that receive the most snow are those areas affected by either a) proximity to the Great Lakes, or b) high elevation. If you are in an area that is affected by both of those factors, then you are almost guaranteed to have a very snowy winter with accumulations in excess of 200 inches! An example of this would be the Tug Hill Plateau, and especially areas in the eastern region. Another example would be the towns located in eastern Cattaraugus County where you are ideally situated to the lee of Lake Erie and you are at a relatively high elevation.

Getting back to elevation, most areas in the Catskill Mountains are at an elevation of at least 1,000 feet, and the highest peaks are around 4,000 feet. The Catskills have a "sweet spot" for heavy snow since they are not only at a high elevation, but they are also far enough west to receive some fringe effects of lake effect snow, and far enough east to receive snow from low pressure systems affecting the East Coast. One of the snowiest towns in the Catskills is Walton, located at the far western edge at a relatively high elevation of approximately 1,200 feet. Walton is also surrounded by mountains which tend to attract snow like a magnet, and because of this, the town can receive upwards of 125 inches of snow each winter! As one drives east from Walton on Route 206, you crest the summit of Bear Spring Mountain (nearly 2,400 feet in elevation) and an annual winter might see 150 inches of snow in this location! Nearly all locations in the Catskill Mountains will see upwards of 90 inches of snow per year, but the highest peaks are likely to receive 150-200 inches!

Another location in Upstate New York that is famous for snow is Old Forge, located in the far southwestern corner of the Adirondack Mountains. Wikipedia indicates that the town has an elevation of 1,857 feet, and if one glances at a map, you can see that Old Forge is located about 80 miles directly east of Lake Ontario. This is the ideal setup for heavy snow in the winter! As such, it would not be uncommon for Old Forge to receive in excess of 225 inches of snow in any given winter! In fact, Wikipedia indicates that the average annual snowfall in this town is just shy of 195 inches!

This part of New York is famous for its spectacular forested landscape among several large lakes, and today Old Forge is known for having the largest water park in the state. The town has also been dubbed the "snowmobiling capital of the

East". Other towns may argue against this honor, but no doubt the terrain of Old Forge is absolutely perfect for winter recreation of any kind.

We should also give some mention to Syracuse ("the cuse") and the amount of snow that it can receive. After all, they don't call it America's snowiest city for no reason! Let's take a look at some snowfall stats for the city of Syracuse, which is home to 145,000 residents, and the greater metro area has more than 700,000 residents. Earlier in this book, I had mentioned that Syracuse receives an annual average of 116 inches of snow. Some sources have it at more than that, such as a website called "Current Results" which says that Syracuse averages 124 inches.

Let's break that figure down by month. First, it is not uncommon for snow to fall during the month of October, but in general, the first accumulating snow arrives by mid-November, and for the month, Syracuse normally receives in the vicinity of 10 inches. In December, the action really gets going and the city will average a whopping 33 inches! January, however, is the snowiest month on average with over 34 inches falling while February comes in third place at 25 inches. Even March can be very snowy with an average of 18 inches, and in some years, much more. Let's take 1993 for example, when the famous Blizzard of '93 dropped 44 inches of snow on Syracuse during the middle of that month over a four-day period! In fact, Syracuse received more snow during this amazing weather event than any other city in the United States. But the snow isn't done in March, necessarily, as April normally averages another 4 inches! When adding all of that up, it comes to 124 inches, which is quite impressive!

Now, let's take a look at the number of snowy days that Syracuse averages each winter. It comes to nearly 70, but only half of those, or 35 days, result in accumulations of greater than one inch. If you want to talk about the number of days that there is snow on the ground, it comes to 78 with depths of at least one inch, while 38 days feature depths of at least five inches. Only 15 days feature snow depths of at least 10 inches, which is not all that bad when you stop to think about it. These

statistics courtesy of
www.currentresults.com.

A few other interesting weather facts about Syracuse is that during the month of February back in 1958, the city had its snowiest month on record with 72.6 inches! Eight years later in 1966, the city had a crippling blizzard that dropped 42.3 inches of snow. The city has also had some extremely cold and snowy winters just recently, and February of 2015 was one of the coldest and snowiest on record. Halfway through the month, the city had received 39.6 inches of snow, and then on the 16th, the mercury dropped to a record low of -17. However, just an hour's drive up Interstate 81 the temperature dipped to a bone chilling -36 in Watertown! Keep in mind these are actual air temperatures, not wind chill. The all-time record low in Syracuse is a numbing -26 set in 1979! However, that pales in comparison to Watertown which dropped to a frigid -43 in January of 1994!

One other extremely snowy area in Upstate New York which was previously mentioned, although briefly, is Fulton, which is only a short drive northwest of Syracuse and located approximately halfway between that city and Oswego. Perhaps no other area is so ideally situated for heavy snow as Fulton is. This small city with a population of approximately 12,000 residents receives some incredibly heavy snow and averages well over 150 inches per season. Let's take a look at some of the averages which have been provided courtesy of tsoforecast.com. This website shows a nice bar graph of snowfall totals for the years 1995 through 2016. The snowiest winter during that period was 1995-96 with 274 inches! The least snowy was 2011-12 with 93 inches.

Now, let's compare Fulton with Syracuse, as the gap in snowfall totals between the two cities is quite wide. Let's take a look back at 1995-96 where Fulton received 274 inches but Syracuse "only" received 171 inches, a difference of 103 inches! If you consult your road map of New York State, you will see that only thirty miles separate these two cities, so the difference in snowfall for such a short distance is quite amazing. The second snowiest winter in Fulton during the twenty year study previously mentioned was 2003-04 where

Fulton received 254 inches, while Syracuse received 181 inches that winter. A difference of 73 inches separated the two cities that winter. In my opinion, the snowiest "city" in Upstate New York is Fulton, without a doubt, but if you are just talking about larger cities, then the award goes to Syracuse, hands down!

One of the most common misnomers regarding snow in Upstate New York is that many people believe the farther north you go, the more snow you will receive. This is 100% incorrect. In fact, some of the most northernmost towns in New York State are the least snowy. Some of the towns that fall into this category are Massena, Malone, Potsdam, and Plattsburgh. The reason why is quite simple. This part of New York is not subject to lake effect snow and is also too far north to receive much snow from low pressure systems along the East Coast. Average annual snowfall in any of these four locations will generally be 45-75 inches per year. However, what they lack in snow they make up for in very cold temperatures!

Speaking of cold temperatures, if anyone is curious to know what the coldest temperature on record is in Upstate New York, it is -52 in Old Forge back in February of 1979. At this temperature, exposed skin is subject to frostbite in just five minutes! My guess is that there were probably several feet of snow on the ground when this record originated, simply due to the fact that some of the coldest temperatures are created at night when radiational cooling takes place. Ideal weather conditions for this to happen include three ingredients, which are a) clear skies, b) little to no wind, and c) snowpack of at least one foot.

In keeping with the subject of snow, perhaps it is worthy to mention the areas in New York State that receive the least amount of snow. I would classify those areas as a) the greater New York City area to include all of Long Island, b) the Hudson River Valley (especially from Kingston south), c) the St. Lawrence River Valley, d) the Lake Champlain lowlands, and finally, e) the Chemung River Valley near Elmira. Most of these areas average between 25-50 inches per winter, but it is not uncommon to receive more.

Well, by this point in time, you have probably learned a whole lot about a subject that may or may not be interesting to you, but as a weather geek, it has certainly been a lot of fun writing this book and being able to share my knowledge of lake effect snow in Upstate New York. One thing is for certain, and that is the fact that if you like snow, then certain parts of Upstate New York are definitely a great place to live! With that said.....LET IT SNOW!!